D1327064

THE

PEASANTRY

OF

THE BORDER:

AN

APPEAL

IN

THEIR BEHALF

BY W. S. GILLY, D.D.,

VICAR OF NORHAM AND CANON OF DURHAM.

NEW INTRODUCTION
BY PROF. R. H. CAMPBELL

GIVE THEM GOOD COTTAGES, AND HELP THEM
TO EDUCATE THEIR CHILDREN.

BRATTON PUBLISHING LIMITED
EDINBURGH

Published by
Bratton Publishing Limited
35 Moray Place
Edinburgh EH3 6BX

First published 1842
© This edition Bratton Publishing Limited 1973

ISBN 0 85975 003 5

Printed in Great Britain by
T. & A. Constable
Edinburgh

ADVERTISEMENT.

It was the original intention of the Author of this pamphlet to prepare a paper, to be read before the Committee of the Highland and Agricultural Society, at their Meeting at Berwick; but he has thought it more convenient to adopt the present form of communicating his statements, and of requesting attention to the Statistical Tables by which they are illustrated, (drawn up with the assistance of Mr. Richard Forsyth,) under the hope that they may be well considered previously to the meeting, and that they may lead to some resolutions beneficial to the peasantry of the country.

Norham, Sept. 17th, 1841.

INTRODUCTION

BY

Professor R. H. CAMPBELL

W. S. Gilly's pamphlet, first published at Berwick-upon-Tweed in 1841, and given a second edition in London the following year, has to be read in the general context of an awakening interest in sanitary conditions. New problems of pollution and infection followed the concentration of people into the new industrial areas in the late eighteenth and early nineteenth centuries. Though the evidence is statistically defective by modern standards, it is not surprising that the death rate rose in the second quarter of the nineteenth century, particularly in the most overcrowded parts of the growing towns, and so reversed the downward trend of previous decades. That fearsome warning lay behind the increasing concern with sanitary conditions which led to the creation of the office of Registrar-General in 1837, and so to the compilation of more accurate vital statistics, and to the general concern represented by the publication in 1842 of Edwin Chadwick's *Report on the Sanitary Condition of the Labouring Population of Great Britain*.[1]

The condition of housing must be considered in any discussion of the sanitary problem, but the exact form of its contribution to the problem is less easily determined. The density and the extent to which houses were serviced with such facilities as adequate drainage, water-supplies and ventilation must be taken into account as well as their size and structure. High density and inadequate or inefficient servicing were particularly harmful in the growing conurbations in which an increasingly large number of people lived in the nineteenth century. Rural conditions were different. Gilly's concern with that aspect of the general problem gives his essay its special significance, for housing in the countryside is not so well documented as in the towns. The reason is not hard to find. The problems of the towns were often more obvious visually, especially to the more articulate and more literate, and their novelty inevitably roused the attention of all those who were interested in such matters. By contrast, some of the defects of rural housing were of long standing, and so were easily accepted, while these very defects sometimes gave rise to quite unintentional, unplanned, and often unwanted benefits. In a reference to Gilly's work in the *Sanitary Report*, Chadwick drew attention to one such matter.

'In the rural districts the very defects of the cottages which let in the fresh air, in spite of all the efforts of the inmates to exclude it, often obviate the effects of the overcrowding and defective ventilation. It has been observed, that while the labouring population of several districts have had no shelter but huts, similar to those described by Dr Gilly, as the habitations of the border

1   See edition by M. W. Flinn, published by Edinburgh University Press, 1965.

peasantry, which afforded a free passage for currents of air, they were not subject to fevers, though they were to rheumatism; but when, through the good intentions of the proprietors, such habitations were provided as were deemed more comfortable from excluding the weather effectually, but which, from the neglect of ventilation afforded recesses for stagnating air, and impurities which they had not the means or had not a sufficient love of cleanliness to remove; though rheumatism was excluded, febrile infection was generated.'[2]

The origins of Gilly's pamphlet are explained in its early pages. The Highland and Agricultural Society (founded as the Highland Society in 1784) encouraged improvements in agriculture and in rural life generally, particularly through providing the incentive of prizes and premia for new ideas and suggestions. Gilly used the opportunity of a meeting at Berwick to encourage the Society to try to improve rural housing on the Border. He was particularly anxious to provide better housing for the full-time agricultural worker, known in Northumberland and in parts of Scotland, as the hind. The absence of any villages, so typical of Scotland, required the hind's employer to provide him with a cottage, but, as it formed part of the fixed capital of the farm, the responsibility was thus transferred to the landlord. Gilly recognised that his plea for improvement would succeed only if he persuaded the landlords to adopt his suggestions, and so his plea was directed to them. Chadwick thought likewise in his *Sanitary Report*.[3]

The issues raised by Gilly were not confined to Northumberland, or even the Border, but were common to a large part of Scotland. His case is based, however, on a detailed exposition of the life of the agricultural worker in the Border parish of Norham, of which he was vicar. His office accounts for some of the more emotional emphasis of the essay, an emphasis which may grate on modern readers, but it also accounts for his intimate knowledge of the life of the parishioners. Gilly considers two paradoxes based on that intimate knowledge: first, the 'Border peasant' was 'intelligent, orderly, and thrifty', yet he did not remain long in the same place; second, he was 'anxious that his children should . . . be instructed in the usual routine of school learning . . . [and] . . . have a *Christian* education', yet their attendance at school was irregular and unsatisfactory. Gilly dealt with the paradoxes very simply—'give them good cottages, and help them to educate their children'.

The pamphlet is an exposition of the paradoxes and of the solution. The argument is based on statistics from Norham, and has illustrations of both improved and unimproved housing, one of which found its way into Chadwick's *Sanitary Report*. The possibility of generalising from the experience of one parish is, of course, limited, but the essay is of value to the historian for its rare insight into the conditions of rural education, and especially of rural housing when the sanitary conditions of the towns were attracting public attention.

2 Chadwick, *Sanitary Report* (ed. Flinn) p. 196.
3 Chadwick, *Sanitary Report* (ed. Flinn) p. 298.

CONTENTS.

PEASANTRY

OF

THE BORDER.

THE great meeting of the Highland and Agricultu- ral Society at Berwick affords me an opportunity of drawing attention, with more than ordinary hope of success, to the condition of the Agricultural Labourers, and of proposing some plans for the improvement of it. Many hundreds of landlords and tenants, eminently distinguished for their benevolence and intelligence, will shortly assemble together, from all parts of the kingdom, for the avowed purpose of communicating and receiving information, on subjects connected with the advancement of agriculture as a science. They will offer, severally and collectively, their contributions of knowledge, as to the best means of improving

4

the breed of cattle, of increasing the productive-
ness of the land, and of multiplying and perfecting
implements of husbandry. Many of the arts and
sciences—especially chemistry, geology, and me-
chanics, and the experience and observations of
our ablest philosophers, theorists, and experimen-
talists, in the use of them—will be brought to
bear on the grand objects of the meeting. We
shall hear of the beautiful state of perfection to
which horses, cattle, and sheep have been brought,
by paying attention to their nature, wants, and
habits. We shall be told of the means that have
been resorted to for the purpose of improving live
stock, as far as regards food, warmth, shelter,
cleanliness, and the prolongation of life. We shall
hear, also, of premiums awarded, and of much that
has been done for draining * and cleansing the
land, for augmenting its produce, and for making
it yield things of the best quality, and in the largest
quantity. In fact, everything, "after its kind,"
which belongs to the cultivation of the land, will
be considered with a view to the great command
—" Be fruitful and multiply." That MAN, the
the first glorious object of creation, may have his
due place in the deliberations of such an assembly,
—that the grand implement on which all depends,

* It is to be wished that the system of *draining* were extended to the
ground on which cottages stand, and to the paths which lead to them.
While nuisances of all kinds—pools of fetid water and sloughs—convey
their noisome vapours to the very threshhold of our labouring population,
the lanes and paths by which they should be approached are rendered
almost impassable by mud and mire.

man's hand, may not seem to be disregarded,—that the workman, on whom the success of every improvement in agriculture depends,—that he, the husbandman, the shepherd, or the herdsman, under whatever name or employment the agricultural labourer be designated,—may have his interests consulted, and his condition improved amidst the general competition in matters of agricultural reform, I venture to submit a few statistical facts to consideration.

While some are directing attention to the flora, An appeal for the peasant. to the minerals, or to the romantic localities of this fine Border District, and others to the better fabrication of various tools and instruments, to the construction of cow-byres, pig-styes, and sheepfolds, and to the irrational animals that are to occupy them,—I will follow the example which has been set by benevolent members of the Society, and beg a few minutes' thought, in behalf of the cottager and the tenement which is prepared for him ; and of the provision which ought to be made for the culture of his mind, and for the advancement of his comforts, as a moral and immortal being.* Let us be doing as much for " right minded man" (to use Sir Robert Peel's term) in his cottage, as we have done for the ox in his crib,

* " No toast is received at these meetings with more enthusiasm than ' *The Peasantry*,' and a more gratifying communication could not be made than that the plan of the Society for improving their domestic comforts continues to give promise of success."—See *Remarks on Cottage Premiums.*

or for the horse in his stable ; let us take care to lodge our peasants as well as we lodge our beasts. And where shall we find a nobler specimen of his kind than the peasant of Tweedside, and of Northumberland in general ? For whether we consider the mental or physical qualities of our northern cottagers, they equally commend themselves to our kindest sympathy and most admiring notice.

The first thing which should be improved in the condition of our northern peasantry is their habitations. The Highland and Agricultural Society have not been inattentive to this desideratum ; for many years they have made the domestic comforts of the peasantry an object of much solicitude, as their reports testify ; and the " Cottage Premiums," and " Garden Premiums," offered by them, have produced the happiest results. (See *Appendix* 1.)

Flitting. Owing to some cause or other—perhaps to a combination of causes—the Northumbrian cottager can scarcely be said to have a *home*, in that delightful sense of the word which is familiar to English ears, and which finds a response in every Englishman's heart. We must give him a *home*, and endear his home to him. It is too much his custom to change his dwelling place ; or, in the language of this region, " *to flit.*" Among the *hinds* * there are not many to be found who were

---

* The hind is an agricultural servant, whose engagement generally lasts for a year, and for whom a cottage is provided by his employer during the period for which he is hired. He is also bound to find a woman to perform field work.—See *Appendix* 2.

born in the parish where they are at present employed; and very few are there, who drew their
first breath in the cottage which is now assigned
to them, or even on the property which they en-
rich by the sweat of their brow. They are hired,
for the most part, from year to year, on an agree-
ment, which binds them to their employer for
twelve months, beginning and ending about Whitsuntide; and as they are governed in their compact with the farmer very much by the employment, which they can obtain for some of their
children as well as for themselves, their continuance in a place depends, in a great measure, on the
arrangements which can be made in reference to
their children. We, therefore, frequently observe
an industrious and well-conducted hind quitting the
service of a farmer, under whom he has been living
with mutual satisfaction, as soon as his children
begin to grow up.

This I consider to be one reason why so many State of the cotta-
of the cottages are such miserable hovels. The ges.
proprietor is not so anxious to provide suitable
abodes for the hinds, as he would be if they were
more stationary; and the hind himself, having an
eye to future change, does not bargain, as he
otherwise would, for the condition of his cottage.
Be it, however, as it may, it is an evil of great The evils of frequent
magnitude that your agricultural people should be change, or flitting,
to the hind.
a moving population. It is an evil to themselves;
they lose all the advantages which belong to *home*,

and the feelings of *home*; they do not share in the benefit of those patriarchal attachments which unite landlord and tenant, employer and servant, neighbour and neighbour, where they have dwelt long together, and have learnt to estimate each other.

The instruction which they receive, be it religious or educational, is interrupted. Many of the little household and garden comforts which they might otherwise get together, whether for use or ornament, are lost or never obtained, because they are about to "*flit.*" He has "no fruit-trees and no flowers in his garden, because he is a *hind*, and may soon be flitting," was the remark made to me a few weeks ago. They are deprived of the opportunity of making friends of the village squire or clergyman; and of procuring those attestations to character which can only grow out of long acquaintanceship. A rolling stone gathers no moss. Character is a working man's fortune. It is the capital with which he begins life.

The evils of flitting to the farmer. The evil to the farmer and to the proprietor is of a similar kind. The removal of the hind's family takes place at an inconvenient and busy season. You scarcely know what it is to be surrounded by an attached and well-known peasantry. "The old familiar face," and the smiling looks of a race of children, whose fathers lived under your fathers, and whose fore-elders worked for your grandsires, and who feel an hereditary and natural affection for you as soon as they can pronounce your name,—there is a pride and pleasure in this to which most of our northern thanes and farmers are strangers. There are many old tenants of *farms*, but few of *hinds' cottages*. Some of the finest farms have been held by the same families for several generations, who are proud of saying, "We and our forefathers have been on this property for a hundred years—for two hundred years —for more!" I have indeed met with some few labourers who can say the same. One old man has worked fifty-six years on the same farm; and a hind's wife told me that her family had lived two centuries under the noble house of Chillingham. Another boasted that for a hundred years a farmer's family in the neighbourhood had had the services of her father and forefathers. But alas, how few such instances! I should rejoice, if this disappearance of a hind's family from the cottages that cradled them could be attributed to the happy fact, that they have risen to a higher station in life, and therefore are no longer to be found in the same locality. But no such thing: you may trace them from place to place, at no great distance perhaps, in the same district, in the same hundred or deanery, but not in the same parish, not on the same property. Had they remained longer there, they might have made friends and patrons, and have attained to a degree above their present condition.

Few instances of long continuance in the same cottage, or on the same property.

Such, then, being the case, I believe that every kind of improvement will follow upon an improvement in the cottage of the peasantry. The state of the hind's habitation affects his continuance in the same place, his resources, his comforts, his moral and religious character, the education of his children, and the chances of his advancement in life. This representation I shall proceed to illustrate by a series of village statistics, drawn up in a district which is peculiarly calculated to exhibit the character, condition, and habits of the Northumbrian husbandman. I have confined my statements to my own parish, for the sake of accuracy and exactness.

The parish of Norham, consisting of 14,268 acres, extends seven miles along the banks of of the Tweed, and when it diverges from that noble river, it stretches out towards a fine country, which produces abundance of corn on the surface, and under it lime and coal. The population is mixed, and consists of agriculturists, pitmen, and fishermen, and the last census gave an enumeration of 2934. But my principal business is with the agriculturists, and especially with that portion of them known by the name of *hinds*, or labourers, who are engaged for twelve months, and for whom cottages are provided on the property upon which they work. It is for these *hinds*, and for a better provision for their comfort and welfare, that I am pleading. *That* better provision should embrace

Many improvements would result from improved cottages.

Norham.

convenient habitations for themselves, and cheap education, near at hand, for their children. Norham is divided into eleven townships, and contains 174 cottages, which are held on the hinding system, (I am not including the free cottages, or those which are hired at their own discretion by *daytal* labourers), 83 of these, according to the annexed statistical table No. I., or nearly one-half, have changed inmates within the last two years, 145 within the last seven years, and 156 within the last ten years. That is to say, out of 174 families occupying the cottages which are reserved for hinds, seventeen only have remained stationary for more than ten years—seventeen families only are to be found on the hearths, around which they were sitting in the beginning of the year 1831.

The flittings in 174 hind's cottages.

This is only a sample of the "*flitting*" which is going on elsewhere, and what are the consequences? The aged dame, whom the appointed minister of the Gospel was gradually preparing to meet her final change, moves away with her son and grandchildren, and she hears no more of that voice, which was pouring the glad tidings of salvation into her ears by the side of her lowly stool.

Consequences of "flitting."

The young people, whom the clergyman of the parish had anxiously instructed for confirmation, and whom he was hoping to see at the Sacrament of the Lord's Supper, have disappeared;—they are removed by the annual "*flitting.*" The clever and studious boy, in whom the village

schoolmaster took delight, and who, he fondly
hoped, would do credit to his teaching, at the summer examination, before his school breaks up for
the harvest, is withdrawn at the Whitsuntide flitting. The good little girl, who thought she was
unnoticed when the patronness of the school last
dispensed her rewards and smiles, and who said—
" Won't you stroke my head too ?"* is now looked
for in vain among the merry group,—her family
have " flitted." And this is the way that the dear-
est associations are broken up, that the deserving
and humble poor are removed from the influence,
which might be beneficial to them here and here-
after, and that an unnatural severment takes place
between the classes in rural life, which should be
most known and most endeared to each other.

Let us now take a closer survey of the localities
and cottages, which have seen such changes within
a few years.

Situation of the
hind's cottages.

They vary in situation, but for the most part I
should say, that they are favourably situated, and
offer every facility for the purpose of being drained, cleansed, ventilated, and supplied with garden
ground, water, and materials of improvement.
Some of them are charmingly placed, embowered
among trees, or commanding beautiful views, and
some on sloping banks, overhanging running
streams. Here might be the cottage garden in

* A fact.

perfection, the village green, and the bowling What a village ought to be. green, the fountain, and the seat under branching trees, where the fathers and mothers might sit and chat in the summer evening, while their children played around them.

To see what a village in our northern regions may be, and ought to be, go to Etall.* There Etall. you will find flower-gardens in perfection — with the village-green, as smooth as a lawn in the best kept pleasure-ground, and the rustic benches under the spreading branches of elm and sycamore. One fine tree, with the seat around its trunk, is conspicuous, with an inscription, which shews the considerate kindness of the noble family, now residing in the mansion house,—" Willie Wallace's Tree." I believe the old man is still alive in whose honour the tree is thus devoted to longevity. But it is to the flower gardens in front of the cottages at Etall to which I am anxious to direct attention, because, as a French author says, " It is the cultivation of flowers which announces a change in the feelings of the peasantry. It is a refined pleasure making a way for itself through grosser materials, like the first opening of the eyes, —it is the perception of the beautiful,—a new sense awaking in the soul. Those who have wandered through country scenes can testify, how the

---

* Etall, in the Parish of Ford, tho residence of Lord Frederick and Lady Augusta Fitzclarence, who are doing everything they can to promote cottage, garden, and educational improvements.

rose tree at the window, or the honey-suckle at the door of a cottage, always promise everything that is delightful within, and a welcome to the weary traveller; for the hand that cultiv..tes flowers never shuts it at the prayer of the destitute or the wants of the stranger. In all countries women love flowers, and make bouquets of flowers, but it is only in the midst of comfort that they conceive the idea of adorning their dwellings with them."

But where the natural landscape is exhibited in such delightful aspects, and where the Lord of All has graciously gladdened the scene with his bounteous hand, we want more examples like that exhibited at Etall, where the moral pleasure of a country life is thoroughly enjoyed, in promoting the cottager's comforts, and in embellishing his habitation.

Wretched condition of hind's cottages. Of the eighty-three tenements in Norham which have changed inhabitants within the last two years, fifty-four are buildings deficient in all that is necessary to convenience and cleanliness, and yet the greater part are occupied by families, who have done all they can to give them a decent and comfortable appearance. Some of them are mere hovels, absolutely unfit for the peasantry of a civilized country, and threatening to tumble down about their ears. In many, human beings and cows are littered together under the same roof. Of the whole number 174, which I am dis-

No 1. A Hind's Cottage.

J. Gellatly Edin.

N.º 2. *A Group of Hind's Cottages.*

cussing, there are but 27 which have two rooms each, and which are supplied with that convenience which is indispensably necessary to cleanliness and decency.

How often when I have visited these hamlets and cottages, have I been surprised by the contrasts which they exhibited. To look at their exterior,* you would suppose that they were inhabited by a tribe of savages. Enter the doors, and you will behold an apartment amply supplied with household chattels, and smiling with content. The cotter and the housewife have done all for themselves which good management can devise. And, in fact, there seems to be a general contribution towards the well-being of our hinds, except by those who provide their habitations. Thanks to the farmers, they have, for the most part, kind and considerate masters. The reply which a worthy farmer made to me on my asking him what he did to induce his hinds to remain with him, should be characteristic of his order. " I try to make them comfortable, and I overlook little faults in good workmen." I have resided in several counties, but in none have I seen the relation so admirably adjusted between farmer and labourer, as in Northumberland. Thanks to the capitalists and manufacturers, they have good raiment, comfortable furniture, and gay crockery-ware. Thanks

The hind well provided with everything but his cottage.

* See plate 1.

to benevolent societies, they have their little book-
shelves, adorned with bibles, books of devotion,
and tracts and treatises of useful and entertaining
knowledge. And, gratitude to a bountiful Provi-
dence, they have fuel in abundance, and a blazing
hearth. " The barrel of meal wasteth not, neither
does the cruse of oil fail," but alas, they have not
tenements worthy of such families, as are the
pride of our land.

A hind's hovel de-
scribed. Now for a more detailed description of that
species of hut, or hovel, for it is no better, which
prevails in this district. I have a group* of five
such now before my mind's eye ; they belong to
the same property† and have all changed inhabitants within eighteen months. The property is
tenanted by one of the best and most enterprising
farmers in all England. The situation is healthy,
and lovely in the extreme. The site, sloping down
to a running stream, having for its back ground
the blue Cheviots in the distance (on which the
south gables seem to rest, when seen in a certain
position), and some woody banks immediately behind it, presents a picture on which Claude Loraine
would have gazed with enthusiasm. But our own
artist, Morland, would perhaps have been still
more charmed, for such a dilapidated. and pic-

* See plate 2.
† I am happy to say that the proprietor of these hovels of the old fashion is about to replace them by new buildings ; and the encouragement
which he gives most liberally to his tenant in the improvement of his
and will, I trust, be extended to his cottagers.

turesquely miserable set of cabins can scarcely be found.

They are built of rubble, or of unhewn stone, Exterior of the loosely cemented; and from age, or from the bad-hovel. ness of the materials, the walls look as if they would scarcely hold together. The chinks gape open in so many places, and so widely, that they freely admit not only the breath of the gentle Zephyr, but the fierce blasts of the rude Boreas; and the Pyramus of one tenement may whisper his compliments, and almost may put in his whole hand, and press that of the rustic Thisbe in the contiguous hovel. The chimneys have lost half their original height and lean on the roof with fearful gravitation. The rafters are evidently rotten and displaced; and the thatch, yawning to admit the wind and wet in some parts, and in all parts utterly unfit for its original purpose of giving protection from the weather, looks more like the top of a dunghill than of a cottage.

Such is the exterior; and when the hind comes Interior of the to take possession, he finds it no better than a shed. hovel. The wet, if it happens to rain, is making a puddle on the earth floor. (This earth floor, by the bye, is one of the causes to which Erasmus ascribed the frequent recurrence of epidemic sickness among the cotters of England, more than three hundred years ago. It is not only cold and wet, but contains the aggregate filth of years from the time of its first being used. The refuse and dropping of

meals, decayed animal and vegetable matter of all
kinds, which has been cast upon it from the mouth
and stomach—these all mix together, and exude
from it.) Window* frame there is none. There is
neither oven, nor copper, nor grate, nor shelf, nor
fixture of any kind; all these things he has to
bring with him, besides his ordinary articles of
furniture. Imagine the trouble, the inconvenience, and the expense, which the poor fellow and
his wife have to encounter, before they can put
this shell of a hut into any thing like an habitable
form. This year I saw a family of eight—husband,
wife, two sons, and four daughters—who were in
utter discomfort, and in despair of putting themselves in a decent condition, three or four weeks
after they had come into one of these hovels. In
vain did they try to stop up the crannies, and to
fill up the holes in the floor, and to arrange their
furniture in tolerably decent order, and to keep
out the weather. Alas! what will they not suffer
in the winter? There will be no fireside enjoy-
ments for them. They may huddle together for
warmth, and heap coals on the fire; but they will
have chilly beds and a damp hearth-stone; and the
cold wind will sweep through their dismal apartment, and the icicles will hang by the wall, and
the snow will drift through the roof, and window,
and crazy door-place, in spite of all their endea-
vours to exclude it.

The hind's difficulties in these hovels.

* On the improvement of *windows* in cottages. See *Appendix* 3

The general character of the best of the old The prevailing character of the hind's cottage. fashioned hind's cottages in this neighbourhood is bad at the best.* They have to bring every thing with them—partitions, window-frames, fixtures of all kinds, grates, and a substitute for ceiling,—for they are, as I have already called them, mere sheds. They have no byre for their cows, no sties for their Destitue of all convenient fixtures. pigs, no pumps or wells, nothing to promote cleanliness or comfort. The average size of these sheds is about 24 by 16. They are dark and unwholesome.† The windows do not open, and many of them are not larger than 20 inches by 16. And Too small for the hind's family. into this space are crowded eight, ten, and even twelve persons. How they lie down to rest, how they sleep, how they can preserve common decency, how unutterable horrors are avoided, is beyond all conception. The case is aggravated when Utterly unfit for the reception of the female bondager. there is a young woman to be lodged in this confined space, who is not a member of the family, but is hired to do the field-work, for which every hind is bound to provide a female. It shocks every feeling of propriety, to think that in a room, and within such a space as I have been describing, civilized beings should be herding together without a decent separation of age and sex. So long as the agricultural system, in this district, requires the hind to find room for a fellow-servant of the other sex in his cabin, the least that morality and

---

* One of these has tumbled down since this page went to press.
† See *Appendix* No. 4 ; and a medical man's opinion.

decency can demand, is, that he should have a second apartment, where the unmarried female and those of a tender age should sleep apart from him and his wife.*

Last Whitsuntide, when the annual lettings were taking place, a hind, who had lived one year in the

---

* Upon another occasion, I may take an opportunity of pointing out, more plainly, the mischief to which the young bondager, or female servant is exposed, by the present mode of hiring and employing her.

The following observations by a French author, " Education des Mères de Famille, par L'Aimé Martin," will apply to many cases in England :—

" The greatest evil in our rural districts, is the degradation of the female sex, by their employment in labours adapted only to men. In ther childhood they herd the cattle, and assist in all the ruder work, in the harvesting, &c. When married they leave their houses, and work in the fields with their husbands. You see them bent downwards to the earth, like heavily laden beasts of burthen, and in some parts of France they are yoked to the plough, with the ox or the ass, hence their skin is wrinkled, their faces burnt, their features masculine, and they sink into a premature decrepitude more hideous than that of old age.

" And whilst they are working like men, their proper occupations are unknown or neglected. Nothing can be more filthy or more unhealthy than the interior of their cottages, where pigs and poultry dispute possession of the damp floor, the door is sunk in the mud, and the window opens upon the dung hill, and in this dirty hole, with the grunting of the animals, and their unpleasant smell, human beings nightly seek rest from their daily toil. *There* is no voice to welcome them, *there* is nothing to cheer them, the table is unspread, the hearth is cold, and before the woman can think of her husband's supper, or look after her children, she must attend to the stables and feed the cattle. These poor creatures have no notion of cleanliness or comfort, kindness and even affection is unknown to them, if you offer them comforts and conveniences, they reject them as strange and useless. To desire *good* we must be sensible of its value ; and these people know nothing but labour and misery. As examples of this state of things we may cite whole provinces—as Perigord, where the women are in a state of debasement and dirt, that reacts upon the whole family : Picardy and Limousin—where they are treated as an inferior race and serve their husbands at table, but are not permitted to sit down by their side : La Bresse—where they are labourers and beasts of burden : Basse Bretagne,—there men, women, and children, live pēle mēle with their sheep and pigs—and are almost savages. The degradation of women is a proof of brutishness in the men—and brutishness in the men is the reaction caused by the degradation of women. Such is the state of the peasantry in almost the whole of civilized Europe. These are the Idylls and Bucolics of a people calling themselves Christians, and the worst of it all is, that we look upon these things with indifference. Time has habituated us to them, and habit has hardened our hearts— and we see these poor people so insensible to their own degradation, that we never think of relieving it."

hovel he was about to quit, called to say farewell, and to thank me for some trifling kindness I had been able to shew him. He was a fine tall man, of about 45. A fair specimen of the frank, sensible, well-spoken, well-informed Northumbrian peasantry —of that peasantry of which a militia regiment was composed, which so amazed the Londoners (when it was garrisoned in the capital many years ago), by the size, the noble deportment, the soldier-like bearing and the good conduct of the men. I Description of the hind's sleeping space. thought this a good opportunity of asking some questions—Where was he going? and how would he dispose of his large family (eleven in number)? He told me they were to inhabit one of these hinds' cottages, whose narrow dimensions were less than 24 feet by 15, and that the eleven would have only three beds to sleep in—that he himself, his wife, a daughter of 6, and a boy of 4 years old, would sleep in one bed, that a daughter of 18, a son of 12, a son of 10, and a daughter of 8, would have a second bed,—and a third would receive his three sons of the age of 20, 16, and 14. " Pray," said I, " do you not think that this is a very improper way of disposing of your family?" " Yes, certainly," was the answer, " it is very improper in a *Christian point* of view, but what can we do until they build us better houses?"

In justice to this excellent class of persons, the hinds of the Border, I must describe the interior of a cottage, when it is fairly " *put to rights*,"

The hind's cottage described when "red up" or "put to rights." after the occupant has taken possession. My description shall be that which will apply, on an average, to the one apartment of all decent agricultural labourers, where the family is not large. Take into consideration the difficulties with which he has to contend before he can convert his shed into this tidy chamber ; see what he has gathered about him to give an air of comfort and smartness to his humble dwelling; look at the homely but ample provision which he has laid in for his winter supply ; cast your eye over the pages of the books which fill one of his shelves, and when you have done this, you will know something of the habits, and you will be able to estimate the character of the meritorious class to which he belongs. We will suppose that it is in the month of December, when we open his door. At first (in many cases, not all) we are put a little out of humour at finding that a cow is tenant of the space, through which we pass into his " parlour and kitchen and all," but though a smell reaches our nostrils which tells us that all cannot always be clean, where a large animal is stalled, yet it is evident that he takes care to " red up" the place, and keep the cowhouse as distinct as he can from his own part of the house, though no partition wall divides them. It is but a slight wainscot work of his own contrivance, which separates Richard from his cow ; but as soon as we have entered within his own domicile, the general aspect within will gladden our

hearts. There are two beds placed within a framework, which takes up the whole of one side of the
room. In the centre of the framework, and between the two beds, is a door which opens into the
space behind the beds, where many useful articles,
such as pails and tubs, are stowed away, and perhaps, if you look in, you will see another bed on
the floor in the corner. The two bedsteads within the framework are so contrived as to close in
by a sliding pannel. This (the whole being kept
bright and clean by rubbing and washing) affords
an air of nicety and neatness to the room, which
has a pleasing effect; but it is to be wished that
the peasantry would substitute curtains or linen
hangings for this unwholesome fashion. Confined
air is one evil, and the difficulty of approaching
an invalid, particularly when surgical aid is necessary, is another evil.* It may be also added, that
this apparatus sometimes forms a screen, which,
desirable on some occasions is equally objectionable in others. It is hard to persuade a hind and
his family to adopt a different apparatus. They
plead truly enough that many of the cottages
would be intolerably cold, without such beds in
which they might box themselves up. It is also
said that no decency could be observed without
them. Every argument they use is an appeal for
a better order of cottages, and a second room. In

* See *Appendix* No. 4.

some cases I have persuaded cottagers to clear away the whole of the pannels in front of the beds and to substitute curtains, and in two or three cottages I have the satisfaction of seeing curtained and not pannelled beds all round, which are so arranged as to serve for screens and divisions just as well as others. They veil what they ought to veil, but they do not conceal what should not be there. From the pannelled beds, which strikes attention at first entrance, our eye rests on the dresser and shelves of pretty crockery ware, which cover the greater part of another side of the room. Every hind's wife has an especial pride in exhibiting her collection of large blue dishes and plates, some of Staffordshire ware, and others of Delf, intermixed with old china, or porcelain tea-pots, cups, and saucers. I have not unfrequently seen relics of a choice and rare pattern, which old Queen Charlotte herself could have coveted. Then comes the handsome clock in its tall case, and the chest of drawers, sometimes of new wainscoat, sometimes of antique carved work (which again many a collector would like to lay his hands on), and which contains decent apparel for all the family, such as they take an honest pride in wearing on all proper occasions,—and where have we a better dressed population than among the northern peasants? The barrel of meal and the barrel of herrings occupy their place. The rack above displays some goodly flitches of bacon. White

Improved beds.

The hind's dresser and crockery-ware.

The hind's clock and chest.

His provisions.

bread loaves we seldom see. The girdle cake, composed of barley and pease, and the oaten porridge, and potatoes, are the usual substitute for wheaten flour.

Now as to the food for our peasant's mind. One book cannot escape our notice. It is " The big *ha' bible,* ance his father's pride." Few of our hinds are without a family bible with notes, and with it we remark one or two smaller bibles. The wish of good King George is realized in this part of the kingdom at least, viz., that every man in his dominions should have a bible, and that every child should be able to read it. Within the district which has come within my own observation (and my enquiries have been directed to this point) I do not know of one single hind's family which wants a bible, or of a child who has reached seven years of age who cannot read, except in cases of imbecility; the prayer-book, some few other books of devotion, of history, or of useful knowledge, are ranged by side of the bible—and they all shew that they have been frequently read. These spiritual treasures have given a tone to the peasant's language : they have stored his mind, they have comforted him in the hour of trial.

His books and food for the mind.

In common conversation, he will use provincialisms in the use and collocation of words which may grate upon refined ears; but lead him into a serious and religious train of thought and discourse, and then you will discern the majesty of

His bible, and the effects of bible reading.

biblical knowledge—then you will hear him express himself in a manner which none can do but those who are in the frequent habit of reading scripture in *the authorised version.* One uniform version has served for all the bible readers in Great Britain for more than 200 years; and the beautiful harmony arising therefrom is heard as much in the peasant's cottage as in the Queen's Palace. Oh, ye who doubt the full extent of the salutary effects produced by bible reading, I have read your observations upon the undirected use of scripture; I have read them with admiration of the learning and devout sentiments by which they are distinguished; but I cannot be one of your converts, I must continue to differ from you, for never have I understood the message of reconciliation more clearly, and never have I felt the force of "Christian morals" more powerfully, than when I have been conversing with some pious hind, whose principal reading is scripture. I am thinking this moment of a grey headed man of 85, who can no longer see to read, but his memory is good, and he can pour out passage after passage in confirmation of his hopes of acceptance at the throne of grace, through the merits of his Redeemer's atonement. I never leave his cottage without feeling that I have learned something from him. I am thinking, too, of an aged widow, whose parish allowance is one shilling a week in aid of the protection which a married daughter (a hind's

Christian comfort and resignation in the hind's cottage.

wife with a family of her own) affords her. When I sympathise with her, and express my regret that she has so little, she silences my condolence with expressions of contentment and thankfulness derived from the pages and the examples of scripture.

One word more on this part of my subject. The hind's cottage very seldom contains any loose productions,—the vulgar ballad and the ribald jest are not to his taste.

Such is the occupant of the miserable habitation which is usually provided for the peasantry of Northumberland and the Borders of Scotland, and, I am afraid, for the majority of agricultural labourers through the land.

But a more considerate spirit is abroad ; many *The spirit of improvement is abroad.* proprietors are turning their attention to this matter ; and cottages and groups of cottages, are arising in all directions, which do honour to those who provided and built them, and secure the comfort of their inmates. On properties in three or four townships out of the eleven which have suggested these remarks, habitations have lately been built for the hinds, which leave a little only to be desired. In one (Duddo) there is a well built *Some better cottages described.* range of dwellings with a single room only, but this of a good size, and every tenement has its separate byre and pig-sty. In another (Grindon) the whole township is nearly rebuilt ; and each cottage has two rooms, and belonging to it a cowbyre, pig-sty, and that other convenience, the want of which is too general in every village in the North. The want of cielings, however, is still a desideratum in the cottages on this property, which a very little additional expense would supply, and would add materially to the warmth and comfort of them.

The Thornton cottages. But I would request especial attention to the new cottages recently built by the Trustees of Lord Crewe's Institution, on their property at Thornton Park.* The group consists of six cottages. Each has two rooms ceiled, with a small passage between them. The larger is 17 ft. 8 in. by 15 ft. 8 in. The smaller is 15 ft. 8 in. by 10 ft. The height of each room is 9 ft. 3 in., and is ventilated by a window which opens, and is 4 ft. 4 in. high by 3 ft. 2 in. wide. The flooring of the rooms is well laid broad flagging. The principal apartment has a grate, an oven, and a furnace-pot as fixtures. The smaller rooms have a grate only. Besides these, there is a small dairy, pantry, and coal-house to each cottage, and the whole is roofed with slate and spouted. Behind the cottage there is a yard, containing a cow-byre, pig-sty, a convenience of another kind, and an ashe or dung-pit, and in front of it a garden 62 ft. long and 31 ft. wide, planted with four apple trees and one pear tree. The situation has no beauty of scenery to recommend it, but the moral charm is attractive beyond expression. Every comfort, every convenience has been

The moral charm of scenery.

* See plates 3, 4, and 5.

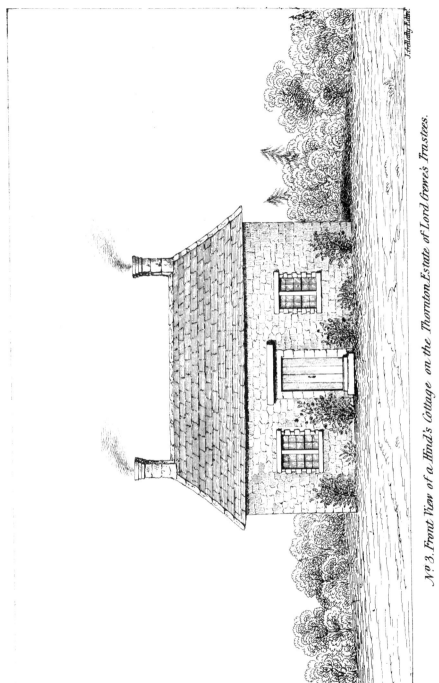

Nº 3. Front View of a Hind's Cottage on the Thornton Estate of Lord Crewe's Trustees.

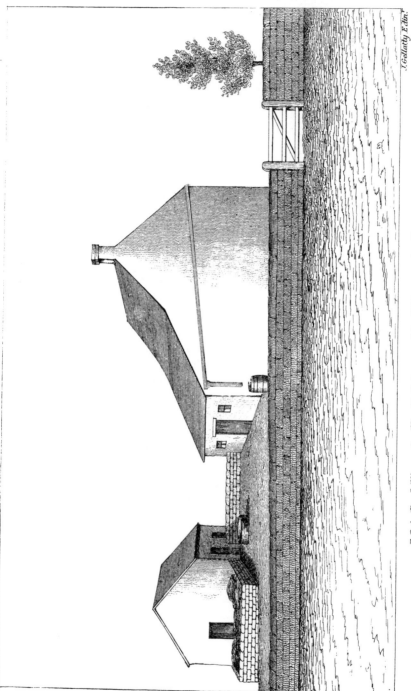

Nº 4. Back View of a Hind's Cottage with Offices on the Thornton Estate.

J.Gellatly E.tin.

supplied, which the benevolence and thoughtfulness of kind hearted landlords could devise, and the whole aspect, (with the capital farm house and offices adjoining, in which nothing that the agriculturist requires is wanting, for himself, his family, his cattle, or the production of his land), is one of cheerfulness and content. The interior of the cottages, abounding in the articles which I have already described, swept and garnished, proves that a good cottage is an invitation to the cleanliness and thriftiness of its occupants; and the fact that hinds continue longer on this property than in most others, speaks equally well for landlords, farmers, and cottagers. The Thornton Park cottages, with their several offices, are more costly perhaps than is necessary: £106, I believe, was the expence of each. An estimate of a cottage with two rooms and sundry conveniences has been shewn me in which the cost is £64.

Suppose £70 to be the average cost of a substantially good cottage, will the comfort of a faithful dependant and his family be heavily bought at this price?* Why is the happiness of rural life to be nothing more than a romance, a poetical image, when it is in the power of so many land-proprietors

---

* In "Remarks on Cottage Premiums," it is stated that Lord Rosebery's improved cottages, with two rooms each, coal-holes, ash-pits, pantries, &c., " generally cost from £75 to £85 a pair, exclusive of carriage. The Marquis of Waterford's cottages at Ford, those of Mr. Cresswell on his property at Cresswell and Bewick, and one which Mr. Donaldson Selby is building for a fisherman in Holy Island, are designed with a view to the cottagers' comfort.

to realize all that is imagined of smiling gardens, and snug habitations, and contented cottagers? The true beauty of a landscape, as Gilpin has said in his Forest Scenery, consists not " in the mere mixture of colours and forms, but in the picture of human happiness presented to our imagination and affections in visible and unequivocal signs of comfort."

Oh, when will the law of love be felt in its supremacy? When will it be felt that there is no security for property like the affection of those whose labour is our wealth?

Often times when I see ornamental lodges, and pretty dairies, like fairy bowers, in a cool and se-questered corner of the park—and gardeners' houses, decorated without, and full of accommo-dation within—and dog-kennels, which may be called canine palaces—and stables, like sacred temples, so totally free from every pollution that you would suppose it profanation to suffer a par-ticle of filth to remain one moment on the pave-ment—often when I see these things do I indulge the ardent hope that the time will come, when the peasantry on a property will have as much taste and forethought expended on them, and that snug cots and happy looking inmates will be considered the chief ornaments of an estate.

Moral culture and improvement.   The moral culture and improvement of the

people is the first of all objects; but as this cannot be attained by means of their habitations only,
we must look a little farther. Among our other
expedients for the amelioration of the hind's condition, in particular, we must endeavour to secure
good education, near at hand, for his children,
and especially for his daughters. The advantages
of female education are not yet sufficiently appre-
ciated or understood. Sewing, mending, and
making, and habits of housewifery so essential to
the character of a cottager's wife, are not to be
learnt in our village schools as they are at present
constituted. A schoolmistress is wanted as well
as a schoolmaster, and if you cannot have one in
every parish or village, at least let there be some
provision made for girls' schools in central spots
for the accommodation of a district, and then you
will see a rapid improvement take place in the
appearance and manners of the female population.
We demand the services of our young females in
the fields, and to counteract the rude tendencies
of field service in females, we should be the more
anxious to educate them in a manner worthy of
their sex. Wherever there is a girls' school, you
are sure to discover its effects in the deportment
and habits both of the children and their mothers.

" There are two ways," says the French author whom I
have already quoted, " of ameliorating the condition of the
peasantry ;—the first is to establish a system of primary instruction on a large scale, *specially* for girls, which shall enable
them at a future time to direct their household affairs, and to
educate their children. To establish in a village the *intellectual superiority* of the women, is to restore to woman that

happy influence which enriches the cottage, and civilizes the people. ' *The education of women is more important than that of men, since the improvement of men is always their work.*' This was Fenelon's doctrine ; and all our legal systems of instruction are defective, because they do not, in the first place and in preference to everything else, provide for the education of girls. No education will ever take deep root in our rural districts if children do not receive it from their mothers, *i.e.* the men from the women. The mother of a family is a moral power, fertilizing the mind, and opening the heart to affection and charity, and every virtue. The second means, and a result of the first, is to give women employment suitable to their sex. This simple change would produce a complete revolution. Restored to their proper place and occupations, woman would regain her proper appearance, and with it her influence—her manners would be softened, her tastes and morals would be purified—she would take delight in cleanliness, she would understand comfort—and in time her husband would be imbued with all her tastes and feelings. The refinement of woman is the greatest check upon the coarseness of man."

Every thing shews that the northern peasantry set a great value on education ; and the statistical tables to which I now request attention prove that

Want of schools more convenienty situated. where good instruction and moderate charges, and the vicinity of a school, invite attendance, there are very few parents who lose the opportunity of sending their little ones to it.

But how can we expect a hind, who is paid in grain,* and whose *money* earnings are therefore but small, to pay 4s. and 4s. 6d. a quarter, or 16s. and

Teachers badly paid 18s. a year, for the schooling of a child, when the school is two, three, and four miles distant, and when the roads or paths to it are almost impassable in bad weather ? And how can we look for good teachers with the miserable pittance which

---

* See *Appendix* 2.

Nº 5. View of a range of 6 Cottages on the Thornton Estate.

No. 2.—POPULATION Statistics of the Parish of Norham.

Townships.	Employment.	No. of Houses	Males.	Females.	Total.	Average to a Family.
Norham, ...	Mixed	193	428	474	902	4·67
Norham Mains,	Agriculturists	22	49	49	98	4·45
Horncliff, ...	Agr.&fishmn.	73	158	164	322	4·41
Loanend, ...	Agricul.	33	60	95	155	4·69
Thornton, ...	Agricul.	31	77	101	178	5·74
Longridge, ...	Agricul.	12	31	37	68	5·66
Shoreswood,	Agr. and pitn.	54	157	158	315	5·83
Felkington,	Agr. and pitn.	26	58	83	141	5·42
Duddo, ...	Agr. and pitn.	50	134	142	276	5·52
Grindon, ...	Agricul.	27	70	73	143	5·29
Twisel, ...	Agricul.	55	160	176	336	6·11
Totals,		576	1382	1552	2934	5.00

No. 3.—NUMBER of Children in Norham Parish between the Ages of 4 and 14 inclusive, who it is considered might attend School, with the number of those actually in attendance.

Townships.	4 Years.	5 Years.	6 Years.	7 Years.	8 Years.	9 Years.	10 Years.	11 Years.	12 Years.	13 Years.	14 Years.	Total in each Township.	No. under Education.
Norham,	32	22	18	19	21	22	12	17	13	17	13	206	184
Norham Mains,	6	3	3	2	4	7	2	1	2	1	2	26	11
Horncliff,	8	9	8	8	8	3	10	8	6	7	3	82	56
Loanend,	3	4	4	1	4	1	2	5	4	1	6	37	19
Thornton,	5	4	8	3	7	7	4	3	3		3	44	36
Longridge,	2	2	1	3	3	3	3	1	8	6	4	22	11
Shoreswood,	13	9	6	13	8	7	7	5	4	1	5	88	59
Felkington,	5	5	5	5	4	3	4	1	8	5	8	42	28
Duddo,	3	9	8	6	9	7	11	6	1	2	4	80	50
Grindon,	4	2	1	6	4	3	5	2	8	8	4	34	21
Twisel,	10	7	6	8	8	5	13	4	8	8	6	83	41
Totals,	91	76	70	74	80	61	73	53	60	52	54	744	516

No. 4.—Table giving a combined view of the Population and Education of Norham Parish, with the charges of the Schools in the vicinity of each Township.

Townships.	Total population.	Average to a Family.	No. between 4 & 14 yrs. of age.	No. receiving Education.	Per Cent. of Population under Education.	Per Cent. of those betw. 4 & 11 under Education.	Average quarterly fees of Schools in the vicinity.	
							Boys' School.	Girls' School.
Norham	902	4·67	206	184	20·40	89·32	3s. per qr.	1s. 2d. per qr.
Norham Mains	98	4·45	26	11	11·22	42·30	3s.	1s. 2d. per qr.
Horncliff	322	4·41	82	56	17·39	68·29	4s.	
Loanend	155	4·69	37	19	12·26	51·35	4s.	
Thornton	178	5·74	44	36	20·22	81·81	3s.	
Longridge	68	5·66	22	11	16·18	50·00	4s.	
Shoreswood	315	5·83	88	59	18·73	67·04	3s. 6d.	
Felkington	141	5·42	42	28	19·85	66·66	4s. 6d.	
Duddo	276	5·52	80	50	18·12	62·50	4s.	
Grindon	143	5·29	34	21	14·68	61·76	4s. 6d.	
Twisel	336	6·11	83	41	12·19	49·39	4s. 6d.	
Total	2934	5·09	744	516	17·58	69·35		

No. 6.—ANALYSIS of the Instruction afforded in Norham Endowed School from November 1840, to May 1841.—Six months.

Reading on Cards and First Class Books,	19 ⎫	
Do. Testament (Junior Class), .	10 ⎭	29
Testament, Miscellaneous Reading Book, and Writing, ...		33
Arithmetic, under Vulgar Fractions, .	18 ⎫	
Do. between Fractions and Mensuration, ...	14 ⎪	
Do. Mensuration, Land Surveying, &c.	7 ⎬	
Do. Trigonometry and Algebra,	4 ⎭	43
Total, . · . . .		105

Six of the above have been instructed in Euclid's Elements.

Eight	...	...	...	Latin.
Twenty-one	..	...	...	English Grammar.
Thirty-six	...	...	...	Geography.
Forty-three	...	...	...	Bible and History of England.
All	...	..	...	Religious knowledge.

No. 5.—COMPARATIVE view of Population and Education in Norham Parish in the years 1831 and 1841.

Townships.	Population in 1831.	Population in vicinity of School,	Population in 1841.	Population in vicinity of School.	Under instruction in 1831.	Under instruction in 1841.	De-crease.	In-crease.	No. be-tween 4 & 14 in 1841.
Norham	782	901	902	1000	152	195		43	232
Norham Mains	119		98						
Horncliff	369	516	322	477	85	75	10		119
Loanend	147	295	155	246	15	47		32	66
Thornton	190		178						
Longridge	105		68						
Shoreswood	279	420	315	456	26	87		61	130
Felkington	141		141						
Duddo & G. Ridge	393	393	276	276	31	50		19	80
Grindon	162		143						
Twisel	302	464	336	479	53	62		9	117
Totals	2989	2989	2934	2934	362	516	10	164	744

they can pick up from children whose attendance is irregular, whose payments are often in arrear, and some of whom occasionally disappear at the annual flitting, and leave them unpaid altogether? There are no functionaries who are so badly paid as the village schoolmaster, where there is no endowment, and no certain remuneration for his services. If a small annual allowance could be secured to help the peasantry in educating their children, and to give the teacher a footing in each village where the population requires a school, the happy effects would shortly be discernible.

The statistical table No. 2 gives a view of the whole population of Norham,* arranged under the several townships, with the average number in each family; and herein it appears that the agricultural townships give the greatest proportion, two of them shewing an average 5.74. and 5.66. and one 6.11. to each family.

Statistical tables.

The table No. 3 exhibits the number of children in each township, between the ages of four† and fourteen, who, it is considered, ought to be receiving education. It classifies the number under the several periods, and presents an enumeration of those who are absolutely under instruction.

No. 4 offers a combined view of the statistics

---

* Norham, with its scattered hamlets and townships, some of them containing above 300 inhabitants, and distant three or four miles and more from the principal village, may be considered a fair sample of a large rural parish,—and shows that the population must not be left to depend on one school for the education of their children.

† In Norham there are twenty-one children of four years of age, and twenty-two of five, attending the schools which are near.

both of the population and of education in the parish of Norham. It exhibits the proportion which the children under education bear both to the whole population, and also to the number of children of a school-going age; and it adds the charges for education made in the school, which is most conveniently situated for the children of each township.

No. 5 presents a comparative view of the state of the population and of education ten years ago, and at the present time. In this table the townships within brackets are so placed to shew the vicinities of the several schools, and the amount of population which would have the benefit of a school centrically situated.

No. 6 exhibits the amount and quality of the instruction communicated, and the number of boys who were receiving their education at the endowed school in Norham village during the six months, 1840 and 1841, when the schools were best attended.

A girls' school, assisted by a fund in aid, is held at the same place. The number in attendance for the same period was about 80, and the more advanced were instructed in needle-work, reading, writing, arithmetic, catechism, religious knowledge, and geography, for one penny a week each, paid in advance.

Proportion of school-going children to the population. It will appear, from an examination of these tables, that out of the whole parish, the greatest number of children receiving education, in proportion to the population, is in Norham township and village, where there are two schools, which have funds in aid of the children's weekly or quarterly payments, and where the schools are conveniently situated for the population. The master of the boys' school has an endowment—a house and £25 a year. The £25 will admit of considerable increase after a certain period. In this township, 184 out of 206, or 89·32 per cent. of the children between four and fourteen, and above 20 per cent. of the whole population are actually receiving education. Next to Norham, Thornton appears to best advantage, 36 out of 44, or 81·81 per cent. of children, and above 20 per cent. of the whole population. Here, also, the school receives the benefit of a fund in aid. Lord Crewes' trustees provide a house and £20 a year for the schoolmaster, with grass for one cow. Horncliff comes third in this order; 56 children out of 82, or 68.29 per cent., and about 17 per cent. of the population. There is a good school-house built in Horncliff by public subscription, which is conveniently situated, and the schoolmaster has an allowance of £10 a year, independent of his quarterly pence. The township, which exhibits the smallest number of children receiving education, in proportion to the total of those between four and fourteen, is Twizel (49.39 per cent. of children, and 12.19 per cent. of population); and there we have nothing to promote instruction. The hamlets of this township are for the most part at a distance from schools, and the charges of those nearest to them, 4s. 6d. per quarter, are beyond the means of the hinds. In one hind's family that I could name, belonging to this township, there are now five children of the several ages of 13, 11, 9, 6, and 4. To provide schooling for the whole of these at 4s. 6d. per quarter, during the two quarters when there is but little field work for the two elder, would take £2, 5s. out of the hind's money payment, which amounts only to £4.* A few years ago, I found another hind's family in another township who reported five of their children as being then actually at school, at a payment of from 3s. 6d. to 5s. a quarter for each; but they all continued at school for a short time only. Had they regularly attended school for the whole year, the expence would have absorbed all the hind's money payment.

Irregular attendance at the schools.

Taking the whole parish of Norham, I find that, upon an average, each child, reported as receiving education, does not attend school more than 22 weeks in the year. This is to be attributed, first, to the field-work which calls them away at certain seasons; and secondly, to the inability of the parents to find the means of paying for their education; and thirdly, to the distance of some of these schools from their habitations.

To exemplify the irregularity of attendance

* See *Appendix* 2.

owing to these causes, I have looked over a village schoolmaster's list, and his accounts for one year In these I find against the name of a family who professedly had four children at school, the sum of 15s. 9d.

				s.	d.
Against the name of another who had 5 children at school,	-	-		9	9
...	...	...	2	8	2
...	...	...	2	10	8
...	...	...	1	3	0
...	...	...	4	16	4
...	...	...	2	6	4
...	...	...	1	5	8
...	...	...	3	6	9
...	...	...	2	5	0
...	...	...	2	3	2
...	...	...	2	4	6

Now how are these evils to be remedied? How are these obstacles to education to be removed? I trust the time will come when some general national plan will be adopted to promote education universally throughout the realm, in conformity with the National Society. Until the consummation of an object so desirable, the parliamentary grant dispensed by the Privy Council, and the Diocesan Societies for Promoting Education will assist largely in constructing school-houses. The building expense varies according to place and circumstances. In the calculations made by Mr. Sinclair, the very able and efficient Secretary of the National Society, taking 50 schools, containing

What can be done to promote education in rural districts.

about 100 children each, the average cost for the buildings was £151, 18s. Smaller schools have been erected for from £92, 10s. on an average, to £61, 15s. In Duddo, a township of Norham, a school of 24 ft. by 15 ft. has been built for £30. The school-master's house, of the same dimensions for the same sum. The stone was quarried on the spot, and the materials were carted gratuitously.

School houses to be conveniently situated.

First, then, we must look out for sites for school-houses, conveniently situated for each branch of the population, and then we must provide a fund in aid for the schoolmaster, to make him up a salary of £50 a-year, and to put the attendance of the children on a better and more regular footing. My statistical tables tell me that a parish of 15,000 acres in extent, to take round numbers, contains a population of about 3,000, and that about a fourth of the whole population, or 750 children, are of an age to be educated. Six schools, well placed, would be required to afford ample facilities of instruction for the children of the several localities of a parish of this extent, at the rate of 125 to each school. I have an account before me, —a list of 93 school-going children belonging to 56 families of a mixed population, and the charge against them amounts to £27, 14s. 3d., *i. e.* 9s. 11d. per family, or 5s. 11d. per child. According to this statement, the average number of children in each family attending school is 1⅔ nearly. But in one agricultural hamlet, I find a group of five cot-

Stipend fund to be provided for teachers.

Number of school-going children in proportion to extent of parish and to the population; and how much can be paid for education by the hinds.

tages, and therein the five families have 11 children of a school-going age, *i. e.* 2 1-5th to each family. The utmost that a hind can conveniently pay, is one penny a-week for each of his school-going children, or 4s. 4d. a-year for each. Let a scheme be prepared and adopted, so that every family may pay 4s. 4d. a-year for each school-going child, by quarterly payments in advance. This will give about £27 a-year to the schoolmaster, supposing him to have 125 scholars on his list. But he ought to have £50 a-year. According to the National Society's Report, 40 schools, containing on an average 88 scholars each, gave the masters a salary of £47, 8s. 6d.

Land proprietors to supply the deficit.

How is the remaining £23 to be made up? By a contribution from the proprietors of the land for the benefit of the peasantry employed on their estates. Six times £23 or £138 would be required from the landed property of a parish of 15,000 acres, which, if assessed at £15,000, would be 2¼d. in the pound, or 18s. 5d. in the £100, and so on in proportion to extent and population. By a provision of this sort, regular attendance would be secured, especially if the farmers would agree to go to the schoolmasters for the children who are to be employed in field work, taking in routine those, whom he should name according to an established rule, and with a view to the age of the boy whose services are required. Mr. Sinclair thinks that field work might be made available towards the expense of schools. Surely we may expect the same attention to their agricultural labourers, and the same liberality on the part of the landed proprietors, as some of the commercial bodies are displaying. The Lead Company at Middleton Teesdale, for instance, are setting a noble example.

Example. The company have schools, or they *pay masters,* wherever they have workmen. They have a school at Middleton, and all the children are *required* to attend after they are six years old, till the boys are twelve and the girls thirteen. One penny per week is paid by parents for each child at school. After they leave the day school, boys are all required to attend the Sunday school till they can pass a thorough examination in the Bible, when each receives a large Bible as a present from the company. The girls, after going into place, often present themselves for examination, and receive the same reward. The company have also established a library at Middleton, and the workpeople and children have the use of the books gratis. This year they gave new books of the value of £20.

A hint may be taken from the admirable arrangements of the Lead Company of Middleton Teesdale. Where they have not schools, *they pay masters.* This should be done in our small hamlets, where there can be no schools, and where the distance is great from the nearest school. A very small annual allowance, say two or three guineas a-year, would induce one of the better-informed hinds, or one of their wives or daughters, (I know of no hamlet where one such cannot be found), to give evening instruction after the day's work is over, from six to eight in the winter, and from seven to nine in the summer. This is the mode adopted in many places on the Continent.

In the *Educational Magazine* of April 1841, there is an admirable paper by Mr. Sinclair, in which he uses some powerful arguments to persuade landlords to make a better provision for the instruction of the children of the peasantry. " Is there," he asks, " any way in which a portion of your funds can be expended so as more effectually to secure the remainder ? Is there any object more spiritually important, more conducive to the diffusion of Christian faith and hope ? Are there any of your fellow-creatures whom you are more bound to help ? If you pass by them, whom are you to assist ? Are there any, over whom your influence can be more effectually exerted ? Is there any way in which your donation, economically considered, will go farther towards realizing its object ?"

Arguments for the adoption of this, or some such plan.

In the foregoing pages, I have endeavoured to shew the condition, the wants, and character of the

Recapitulation.

Border peasant. It is well known that he is intelligent, orderly, and thrifty, and yet he seldom remains long in one place. He is religiously disposed, and anxious that his children should not only be instructed in the usual routine of school learning, but that they should have a *Christian* education. And yet the attendance of his children at school is irregular and unsatisfactory. My statistical tables establish these two facts, and the statements that I have advanced explain them. He changes his habitation and his service, because the one is a miserable hovel, and the other does not always secure employment for his family. He suffers his children to stay away from school, and to lose the advantage of uninterrupted instruction, because he cannot afford to pay for it, or because the distance from school is inconvenient, and sometimes impracticable. A hind, a parishioner of mine, left his employer last Whitsuntide, after living several years under him, because he could obtain a better cottage, and cheaper education in Bamborough. These frequent flittings, so injurious to the farmer and the hind, are manifestly caused by a discontent of some kind, which is almost universal. I have endeavoured to trace it to its causes, and have suggested two modes of removing the evil. Give them good cottages, and help them to educate their children.

Suggestions. As for the manner and the scale in which they are to receive educational aid, I do not take upon myself to say that the plan which I have submitted to consideration, is one of the best that could be adopted. I have indeed suggested a scheme, and have illustrated it by figures and calculations, but this was to fasten attention to the subject, and to induce others to think, and to reckon up and to count, at how small a cost they might improve the intellectual, religious, and moral condition of the children of their peasantry. At the rate of 18s. 5d. in the £100, you may effectually assist the hinds on your estate to educate their children. That is to say, give £4, 12s. 1d. out of your rental of £500 a-year, or £9, 4s. 2d. out of your rental of £1000 a-year, and you are securing instruction for the children of your cottagers. Should you put this, or anything like it in practice, do it as your own gift, let it be known to come out of your own pocket, and do not make it to be, or seem to be, part of your tenants' rent.

It may be objected that the plan must be generally adopted to render it effective, and that the hind himself must be induced to acquiesce in an arrangement, which will tie him down to pay 4s. 4d. for each child, who is of an age to go to school. Granted. But I believe that land proprietors and peasantry only require to have the benefit of some such system thoroughly explained to them, and to see how it works, in order to give their cordial assent to it. Let a few proprietors set the example of contributing to an educational fund; let a few farmers make a compact with their hinds, that a penny a-week is to be deducted from their earnings for each child who ought to be at school, upon the understanding that they may send all their children to a school near at hand, at this rate of charge, whenever they please: and the course of improvement will soon begin. On an average, according to my statistical tables, each family has about two children of an age to be going to school,—8s. 8d. would therefore be the amount of yearly payment during a variable number of years.

In the same manner, if a few more benevolent persons would commence the undertaking of building new cottages on their estates, and of encouraging their cottagers to cultivate gardens, and to exhibit taste and order in household management, and horticulture, the example would spread far and wide, and our rural districts would soon exhibit that aspect, which is now only the dream of romancers and poets. The woodbine cottage and the bower of roses, and the garden of sweets and of vegetables, and the rich orchard, would, in process of time, grace almost every village and hamlet in merry England. And what is still more desirable, the peasant and his wife, and his children, would rise in manners and in Christian morals, in proportion to the outward comfort about them, and they would elevate their thoughts from the flowers of the garden, and the lilies of the field, to God, who has arrayed those productions of his wisdom and goodness in beauties exceeding the glory of Solomon.

The movement has begun. Cottages are spring- *The commencement of Improvement.* ing up, gardens are blooming, and schools are being constructed, which attest that many lords of the manor are anxious that the " *cottage homes of England*" should be as much the abodes of comfort as their own mansion-houses. I have already alluded to the efforts of the Highland and Agricultural Society; and even while I have been preparing this appeal for the press, a prospectus has been sent to me, which contains " *The outline of general rules for a society supplementary to the agricultural society of the county, to promote the improvement of cottages and cottage gardens in Northumberland.*"

In addition to this happy token for good, an announcement has been made, that many of the leading members of agricultural societies, visitors from a distance, as well as proprietors from each side of the Border, who are expected to be present at the meeting at Berwick, to be held September 29 and 30 and October 1, on the 2d October are invited to partake of the hospitalities at Etall House, in order that attention may be directed to the practical ameliorations which have already been effected, and to those which would farther result, from an extended association to improve the condition of cottages and cottagers.

This is the way to set about the grand work of improvement,—shew what has been done, and what may be done. The sure and never-failing word of God promises, that "The wilderness and solitary place shall be glad, and the desert shall rejoice and blossom as the rose." Man is the agent of God's benevolent intentions towards man, and if we would all consider ourselves as instruments in his hands for the distribution of his bounty, and stewards of the good things entrusted to us for the benefit of those around us, this country of ours would become an earthly paradise. "Who maketh thee to differ from another?" "What hast thou that thou didst not receive?" And why dost thou differ? And why didst thou receive? These are questions which we should all put to ourselves, and then the measure of our liberality, and the extent of our carefulness for those who labour for us, would be upon a very different scale.

The benevolent Hannah More once thought of writing on " *The law of consideration.*" If she had, how much might she have said on the duty of thinking and acting, more than we do, in behalf of the working classes. " I feel persuaded," says Mr. Bosanquet, in his *Rights of the Poor, and Alms-giving Vindicated*, " that an entire change of opinion and feeling towards the classes beneath us, that a total change of conduct must be wrought, before we can lay any just claims to the character of a really Christian people—Christians not in name and in doctrines only, but in feeling and conduct." P. 290. He says in another place, " What the poor most want is a friend. They want more notice, and attention, and communication. The classes are estranged from one another. There is no such connexion as that of patron and client, that the poor man might always have some one person to resort to for advice, for assistance, for protection, for defence, for encouragement in his depression."

" It is in the habits and amusements of life that the poor especially want the countenance, the encouragement, the intercourse, and influence of the rich. An amused and happy people is never a rebellious one."—P. 363.

The intercourse, which Mr. Bosanquet recommends, would fix our regards more closely on that class, without whose daily toil the land would be a wilderness. An examination of the intellectual resources of our peasantry would lead to an improved system of education; and an inspection of their habitations would conduce to a system of cottage building and embellishment, which would promote happiness within doors and amusement without.

But we shall never attend as we ought to the necessities and circumstances of those around us, nor shall we devote a sufficient portion of our consideration and of our substance to the benefit of

The Christian standard.

others, until we are more thoroughly convinced, by divine influence, that we all fall far below the standard of that Christian rule, " *As ye would that men should do unto you, do ye also to them likewise.*"

" If it shall ever please God to shew, on a large scale, what the world, in which man is placed, might become, if only it were directed in conformity to his revealed will, that result must be wrought by the *Religion of Christ* actuating the hearts and regulating the practice of the community in general ; and the *Religion of Christ*, when it does actuate the heart, will direct the practice to this end ; and unless, in the main, the practice is thus directed, there is occasion for much doubt, and need for much self-inquiry, as to the reality of Christian *Faith.*"*

---

* See Bishop of Chester's preface to " *Christian Charity, its Obligations and Objects with reference to the Present State of Society.*"

APPENDIX

Page 6.
Appendix 1. —" But although a great deal must always
depend on the occupant—and a well-conducted family will
do much to overcome the difficulties occasioned by defective
accommodation—it cannot be denied that in all parts of Scotland the lodging of the peasantry is generally so contracted,
and so destitute of every thing like convenience, as to render
proper or economical arrangement nearly impracticable for
any ordinary tenant. These defects were forcibly noticed by
the Earl of Rosebery, at the general meeting of the Society in
January 1839 ; and, for the information of other proprietors,
his Lordship obligingly allowed the plans and specifications of
the cottages which he has erected upon his own estate to appear in the 44th number of these Transactions. As an in-
ducement to follow so good an example, medals have been
offered by the Society to proprietors for building cottages of
a good construction ; and these medals are already in demand.
This subject was again brought forward by the Marquis of
Tweeddale who filled the chair at the last general meeting ;
and throughout the whole of Scotland it is attracting increasing attention. The style of such buildings is every where
improving, and the measures of the Society will make the
country acquainted with the best models.--*Report of Com. of
High. and Agr. Soc. on Improving the Lodging of the Peasantry.*

"The result is most gratifying,—not only have dung-hills
and all other deformities been generally removed, but in many
cases the fronts and gables of the cottages have been ornament-
ed with honeysuckles, roses, and ivy, the walls being always
kept neatly white-washed, and the wood and sills of the windows tastefully painted. Nor does the exterior belie the ap-
pearances that present themselves within, such attention being

paid to cleanliness and comfort, that whoever chooses to make the trial, will not fail to enjoy the cottage luxury of

' A cheery ingle and a clean hearth-stane.'

In the garden department, the improvement made is scarcely less remarkable. These are generally small, but the most has been made of them, considering their dimensions. They are particularly well kept, and laid out with due regard both to taste and economy."—*Report of Com. on the competition for Premiums offered for Cottages in* 1840.

" It is now clearly established, that the humblest peasant has it in his power to add much to the comfort of himself and his family, by devoting a small portion of his spare time to the work pointed out by the Society. It is seen that when once engaged in this work, it becomes an attractive amusement to which he requires no prompting. It has been shewn that when even a few individuals in a district acquire a taste for such recreations, it presently spreads among their neighbours ; and, finally, it has been distinctly ascertained, that the higher orders, by a due exercise of that influence which they possess, may do much towards forwarding this most important reformation, but that without their aid nothing is to be accomplished."—*Ibid.*

Pages 6 and 36.

Payment in grain. *Appendix* 2.—The following calculation of a hind's earnings was made ten years ago.

He receives in payment for his year's labour—

36	Bushels of	Oats.
24	do.	Barley.
12	do.	Peas or Beans.
3	do.	Wheat.

	£.	s.	d.
Total, 75 bushels of grain—value say	13	0	0
Pasturage or food for a cow through the year. Cows produce	10	0	0
Ground, 1000 yards, to plant 3 bushels potatoes —worth	2	0	0
Coals carted for him, with house and garden rent free—say	3	10	0
Money payment	4	0	0
Total value,	£32	10	0

Value of such payments.

One condition of the hind's engagement is that he finds the services of a woman, called a bondager, who is to work for 10d. a-day in the summer, 8d. a-day in the winter, and 1s. a-day in harvest. This bondager is generally the wife, sister, or daughter of the hind ; or in lieu of one of these, a female must be hired by him.

Bondagers.

3

Wives and children occasionally find employment in the fields or barn, at wages of, to the woman 8d. or 10d. a-day, to the children from 4d. to 8d. and 10d.

Sometimes a father and son are hired together on this hind- ing system, in which case the father's terms are as above. The son receives

24 bushels of Oats,
12 do. Barley,
6 do. Peas or Beans,

with some quantity of ground planted with potatoes, and £11 in money.

This case of a *double hind* in one family is considered advantageous both to the farmer and his labourers.

To reduce the above mentioned system to its value in money, and to exemplify its working in families, I select four cases, and the amount of earnings in each.

I.—Thomes P—— has a wife and six children.

	£.	s.	d.
The earnings and advantages of Thomas as detailed above,	32	10	0
His wife harvesting at 15s. a-week,	3	0	0
Isabella P——, aged 19, living with her father as bondager, earned	9	4	0
William P——, his son, aged 12, earned	5	10	6
Total earnings of his family,	£50	4	6

£50, 4s. 6d.

II.—Thomas B——, wife and seven children.

	£.	s.	d.
Thomas B—— advantages same as T. P.,	32	10	0
Son James, aged 15, earned 4s. a-week,	10	8	0
Daughter Isabella, aged 13, 4s. a-week for eight months,	6	0	0
Son Thomas, 11 years, 2s. 6d. a-week for summer, half year,	3	0	0
His wife having a child could not harvest.			
Total,	£51	18	0

£51, 18s. 0d.

III.—

	£.	s.	d.
A similar mode of calculation give to Esau P——, wife and ten children, earnings, &c., per week,	1	6	6
Total for the year,	£68	8	0

£68, 8s. 0d.

IV.—A hind's usual earnings and advantages when he has not a family sufficiently grown up to earn anything.

	£.	s.	d.
Man's grain, money payment, &c., as above, ⁓	32	10	0
Wife's harvesting, ⁓ ⁓ ⁓ ⁓	3	0	0
Bondager earns, ⁓ ⁓ ⁓ ⁓	9	0	0
	44	10	0
If the bondager is not one of the family, deduct			
her wages ⁓ ⁓ ⁓ ⁓ ⁓	7	0	0
	£37	10	0

£37, 10s. 0d.

Page 18.

Appendix 3.—" The window for which the premium has been awarded to Messrs. M'Culloch & Co. is extremely simple in its construction, and may with safety be pronounced efficient in point of comfort and utility ; while the price, it is believed, will be not higher than the cheapest description of iron windows now in use ; and for durability will be preferable to those of any other material. The dimensions that have been recommended for the windows of ordinary cottages are 39 inches for the height and 24 inches to the width, within the wooden frames. The size of glass required for these frames is $7\frac{1}{4}$ by $5\frac{1}{4}$ inches. The sash is divided into two unequal parts, the lower part having three squares in height, and the upper part two. The lower part is permanently fixed, while the upper part is constructed to turn in the vertical direction on pivots, which are situate in the line of its middle astragal, and both parts are set in a substantial wooden frame, which may be either built in while the wall is erecting, or may be set in afterwards in the ordinary way, with or without *checked rybats* according to the taste of the proprietor."— *Report on Improving the Lodging of the Peasantry.*

Page 19.

Appendix 4.—Letter from Mungo Park, Esq., Surgeon, &c.

" Sir,—As medical officer to the district of Norhamshire, I beg to offer to your notice a few remarks on the sanatory state of the labouring classes in it.

" To maintain the inhabitants of a parish in a healthy state it is of the utmost importance that the houses should be comfortable, affording not only good shelter from the inclemency of the weather, but also suitable conveniences. All stagnant pools of water—ditches, containing filth—and accumulations of refuse thrown from houses or otherwise collected, being obnoxious to health on account of the vegetable and animal matter gathered together and exposed in a state of decomposition, should be drained off, covered in, or otherwise removed. All of these are a source of great evil by their producing a vapour named miasma, which is capable of producing a most injurious effect on the human body—generating intermittent and remittent fevers, &c.

" In many parts of this district the cottages are miserable and unfit to be inhabited. In more instances than one I have remarked in the course of my practice that the inmates of some of the worst Cottages have been subject to fever from no other cause than insufficient shelter. There are also stagnant ditches and pools of water as well as collections of filth in various parts of the district

" In constructing Cottages I would beg to suggest a very necessary improvement in their internal economy viz : That each Cottage should contain more apartments than one, by which the very objectionable use of close beds might be discontinued, as they cannot fail to be extremely detrimental to health, it being no uncommon circumstance for one of these beds to be obliged to contain too many persons at a time : it may also be mentioned that they are also a very great inconvenience to medical men, more especially in cases of accident. It is my opinion that were the plan of extending the Cottager's accommodation adopted, it would prove to be very conducive to the general comfort of the labouring classes — as well as being also highly calculated to improve the morals of this important class of people, and it would also be a source of convenience in case of sickness, when it often happens that it is of the greatest importance for the welfare of the patient that he should have a separate apartment.

" Since I located in the district of Norhamshire (October, 1837) the following diseases have been epidemical, viz., scarletina, small-pox, measles, and influenza ; continued fever and typhus have not been prevalent to any considerable extent, but during the fall of the year there are generally a few cases.

With respect to vaccination, great progress has been made in this department, owing to the facility afforded to the inhabitants of this district by the new act for the extension of vaccination. Since January of this year, two hundred and twenty persons have been vaccinated by me. Some prejudice and neglect still remains, but it is inconsiderable.

" I am, Sir, your obedient servant,

" MUNGO PARK.

" Norham, Sept. 10, 1841."
To the Rev. Dr. Gilly.